FRANCIS FRITH'S

SOUTH DEVON COAST
PHOTOGRAPHIC MEMORIES

THE FRANCIS FRITH COLLECTION

www.francisfrith.com

Francis Frith's
SOUTH DEVON COAST

◆

PHOTOGRAPHIC MEMORIES

Francis Frith's
SOUTH DEVON COAST

John Bainbridge

First published in the United Kingdom in Hardback in 2000 by
The Francis Frith Collection

ISBN:1-85937-107-8 Reprinted in Hardback in 2005
ISBN:1-84589-420-0 Paperback Edition

British Library Cataloguing in Publication Data

South Devon Coast
John Bainbridge
ISBN 1-84589-420-0

Frith Book Company Ltd
Frith's Barn, Teffont,
Salisbury, Wiltshire SP3 5QP
Tel: +44 (0) 1722 716 376
Email: info@francisfrith.co.uk
www.francisfrith.com

Printed and bound in Great Britain

Front Cover: **TORQUAY**, *Anstey's Cove 1896* 38609t

The colour-tinting is for illustrative purposes only, and is not intended to be historically accurate

Aerial photographs reproduced under licence from Simmons Aerofilms Limited.
Every attempt has been made to contact copyright holders of illustrative material. We will be happy to give full
acknowledgement in future editions for any items not credited.
Any information should be directed to The Francis Frith Collection.

AS WITH ANY HISTORICAL DATABASE THE FRITH ARCHIVE IS CONSTANTLY BEING CORRECTED AND IMPROVED
AND THE PUBLISHERS WOULD WELCOME INFORMATION ON OMISSIONS OR INACCURACIES

CONTENTS

FRANCIS FRITH: *Victorian Pioneer*

FRANCIS FRITH, Victorian founder of the world-famous photographic archive, was a complex and multitudinous man. A devout Quaker and a highly successful Victorian businessman, he was both philosophical by nature and pioneering in outlook.

By 1855 Francis Frith had already established a wholesale grocery business in Liverpool, and sold it for the astonishing sum of £200,000, which is the equivalent today of over £15,000,000. Now a very rich man, he was able to indulge his passion for travel. As a child he had pored over travel books written by early explorers, and his fancy and imagination had been stirred by family holidays to the sublime mountain regions of Wales and Scotland. 'What lands of spirit-stirring and enriching scenes and places!' he had written. He was to return to these scenes of grandeur in later years to 'recapture the thousands of vivid and tender memories', but with a different purpose. Now in his thirties, and captivated by the new science of photography, Frith set out on a series of pioneering journeys to the Nile regions that occupied him from 1856 until 1860.

INTRIGUE AND ADVENTURE

He took with him on his travels a specially-designed wicker carriage that acted as both dark-room and sleeping chamber. These far-flung journeys were packed with intrigue and adventure. In his life story, written when he was sixty-three, Frith tells of being held captive by bandits, and of fighting 'an awful midnight battle to the very point of surrender with a deadly pack of hungry, wild dogs'. Sporting flowing Arab costume, Frith arrived at Akaba by camel sixty years before Lawrence, where he encountered 'desert princes and rival sheikhs, blazing with jewel-hilted swords'.

During these extraordinary adventures he was assiduously exploring the desert regions bordering the Nile and patiently recording the antiquities and peoples with his camera. He was the first photographer to venture beyond the sixth cataract. Africa was still the mysterious 'Dark Continent', and Stanley and Livingstone's historic meeting was a decade into the future. The conditions for picture taking confound belief. He laboured for hours in his wicker dark-room in the sweltering heat of the desert, while the volatile chemicals fizzed dangerously in their trays. Often he was forced to work in remote tombs and caves where conditions were cooler. Back in London he exhibited his photographs and was 'rapturously cheered' by members of the Royal Society. His reputation as a photographer was made overnight. An eminent modern historian has likened their impact on the population of the time to that on our own generation of the first photographs taken on the surface of the moon.

VENTURE OF A LIFE-TIME

Characteristically, Frith quickly spotted the opportunity to create a new business as a specialist publisher of photographs. He lived in an era of immense and sometimes violent change. For the poor in the early part of Victoria's reign work was a drudge and the hours long, and people had precious little free time to enjoy themselves.

Most had no transport other than a cart or gig at their disposal, and had not travelled far beyond the boundaries of their own town or village. However, by the 1870s, the railways had threaded their way across the country, and Bank Holidays and half-day Saturdays had been made obligatory by Act of Parliament. All of a sudden the ordinary working man and his family were able to enjoy days out and see a little more of the world.

With characteristic business acumen, Francis Frith foresaw that these new tourists would enjoy having souvenirs to commemorate their days out. In 1860 he married Mary Ann Rosling and set out with the intention of photographing every city, town and village in Britain. For the next thirty years he travelled the country by train and by pony and trap, producing fine photographs of seaside resorts and beauty spots that were keenly bought by millions of Victorians. These prints were painstakingly pasted into family albums and pored over during the dark nights of winter, rekindling precious memories of summer excursions.

THE RISE OF FRITH & CO

Frith's studio was soon supplying retail shops all over the country. To meet the demand he gathered about him a small team of photographers, and published the work of independent artist-photographers of the calibre of Roger Fenton and Francis Bedford. In order to gain some understanding of the scale of Frith's business one only has to look at the catalogue issued by Frith & Co in 1886: it runs to some 670

court card, but there was little room for illustration. In 1899, a year after Frith's death, a new card measuring 5.5 x 3.5 inches became the standard format, but it was not until 1902 that the divided back came into being, with address and message on one face and a full-size illustration on the other. *Frith & Co* were in the vanguard of postcard development, and Frith's sons Eustace and Cyril continued their father's monumental task, expanding the number of views offered to the public and recording more and more places in Britain, as the coasts and countryside were opened up to mass travel.

pages, listing not only many thousands of views of the British Isles but also many photographs of most European countries, and China, Japan, the USA and Canada – note the sample page shown above from the hand-written *Frith & Co* ledgers detailing pictures taken. By 1890 Frith had created the greatest specialist photographic publishing company in the world, with over 2,000 outlets – more than the combined number that Boots and WH Smith have today! The picture on the right shows the *Frith & Co* display board at Ingleton in the Yorkshire Dales (left of window). Beautifully constructed with a mahogany frame and gilt inserts, it could display up to a dozen local scenes.

Francis Frith died in 1898 at his villa in Cannes, his great project still growing. The archive he created continued in business for another seventy years. By 1970 it contained over a third of a million pictures of 7,000 cities, towns and villages. The massive photographic record Frith has left to us stands as a living monument to a special and very remarkable man.

POSTCARD BONANZA

The ever-popular holiday postcard we know today took many years to develop. In 1870 the Post Office issued the first plain cards, with a pre-printed stamp on one face. In 1894 they allowed other publishers' cards to be sent through the mail with an attached adhesive halfpenny stamp. Demand grew rapidly, and in 1895 a new size of postcard was permitted called the

Frith's Archive: *A Unique Legacy*

FRANCIS FRITH'S legacy to us today is of immense significance and value, for the magnificent archive of evocative photographs he created provides a unique record of change in 7,000 cities, towns and villages throughout Britain over a century and more. Frith and his fellow studio photographers revisited locations many times down the years to update their views, compiling for us an enthralling and colourful pageant of British life and character.

We tend to think of Frith's sepia views of Britain as nostalgic, for most of us use them to conjure up memories of places in our own lives with which we have family associations. It often makes us forget that to Francis Frith they were records of daily life as it was actually being lived in the cities, towns and villages of his day. The Victorian age was one of great and often bewildering change for ordinary people, and though the pictures evoke an impression of slower times, life was as busy and hectic as it is today.

We are fortunate that Frith was a photographer of the people, dedicated to recording the minutiae of everyday life. For it is this sheer wealth of visual data, the painstaking chronicle of changes in dress, transport, street layouts, buildings, housing, engineering and landscape that captivates us so much today. His remarkable images offer us a powerful link with the past and with the lives of our ancestors.

TODAY'S TECHNOLOGY

Computers have now made it possible for Frith's many thousands of images to be accessed almost instantly. In the Frith archive today, each photograph is carefully 'digitised' then stored on a CD Rom. Frith archivists can locate a single photograph amongst thousands within seconds. Views can be catalogued and sorted under a variety of categories of place and content to the immediate benefit of researchers. Inexpensive reference prints can be created for them at the touch of a mouse button, and a wide range of books and other printed materials assembled and published for a wider, more general readership - in the next twelve months over a hundred Frith local history titles will be published! The

See Frith at www.francisfrith.co.uk

day-to-day workings of the archive are very different from how they were in Francis Frith's time: imagine the herculean task of sorting through eleven tons of glass negatives as Frith had to do to locate a particular sequence of pictures! Yet the archive still prides itself on maintaining the same high standards of excellence laid down by Francis Frith, including the painstaking cataloguing and indexing of every view.

It is curious to reflect on how the internet now allows researchers in America and elsewhere greater instant access to the archive than Frith himself ever enjoyed. Many thousands of individual views can be called up on screen within seconds on one of the Frith internet sites, enabling people living continents away to revisit the streets of their ancestral home town, or view places in Britain where they have enjoyed holidays. Many overseas researchers welcome the chance to view special theme selections, such as transport, sports, costume and ancient monuments.

We are certain that Francis Frith would have heartily approved of these modern developments, for he himself was always working at the very limits of Victorian photographic technology.

THE VALUE OF THE ARCHIVE TODAY

Because of the benefits brought by the computer, Frith's images are increasingly studied by social historians, by researchers into genealogy and ancestory, by architects, town planners, and by teachers and schoolchildren involved in local history projects. In addition, the archive offers every one of us a unique opportunity to examine the places where we and our families have lived and worked down the years. Immensely successful in Frith's own era, the archive is now, a century and more on, entering a new phase of popularity.

THE PAST IN TUNE WITH THE FUTURE

Historians consider the Francis Frith Collection to be of prime national importance. It is the only archive of its kind remaining in private ownership and has been valued at a million pounds. However, this figure is now rapidly increasing as digital technology enables more and more people around the world to enjoy its benefits.

Francis Frith's archive is now housed in an historic timber barn in the beautiful village of Teffont in Wiltshire. Its founder would not recognize the archive office as it is today. In place of the many thousands of dusty boxes containing glass plate negatives and an all-pervading odour of photographic chemicals, there are now ranks of computer screens. He would be amazed to watch his images travelling round the world at unimaginable speeds through network and internet lines.

The archive's future is both bright and exciting. Francis Frith, with his unshakeable belief in making photographs available to the greatest number of people, would undoubtedly approve of what is being done today with his lifetime's work. His photographs, depicting our shared past, are now bringing pleasure and enlightenment to millions around the world a century and more after his death.

SOUTH DEVON COAST – *An Introduction*

TO TRAVEL ALONG Devon's south coast is to participate in a journey of many delights, whether you undertake the long trek on foot along the South Devon Coastal Footpath, from Plymouth to the Dorset border at Lyme Regis, or go by car or public transport from village to village and town to town.

In spite of its popularity with generations of holidaymakers, much of the coast remains unexplored except by the few. There are great stretches of high cliff, lonely beaches, wild and unspoiled interior countryside and quaint fishing villages to seek out.

Even the city of Plymouth does not yet overwhelm the pastoral countryside of the South Hams, and it has its own delightful walks and dramatic areas of coastline. The increasingly large conurbation of Torbay is still broken up by some attractive pieces of countryside, though these now seem to be under siege from modern development.

In Teignbridge and East Devon we have two of the oldest seaside resorts in the county - Teignmouth and Exmouth. Their layout tells us much about the development of the holiday industry in Britain. They also have the considerable merit of being surrounded by some of the finest scenery along the coast.

The Frith photographers caught these urban and rural landscapes before the character of the towns was compromised by massive building programmes and the dominance of the motor car. But if these pictures are an illustration of things lost, they are also useful pointers to the better parts of the South Devon coast which remain - seek these out and enjoy them.

Plymouth and The South Hams

THE PLYMOUTH WE see today is not the city that residents and visitors would have known before the Second World War. Even by the standards of the worst wartime blitzes Plymouth suffered badly, being devastated beyond recognition. The heart of the old Victorian town was torn out, mostly during one terrible night. All we have to remember the old Plymouth by is archive film, photographs such as the ones that follow, and the memories of survivors.

Not all of the old city was lost. A stroll through the Barbican to Sutton Harbour, which the bombs mostly spared, gives a feel of old Plymouth town as Drake might have known it. But ten thousand other old buildings were destroyed, and seventy thousand more were damaged by high explosive and firestorm. It says a lot for the indomitable spirit of the people of Plymouth that after the

bombing of St Andrew's Church, a painted wooden notice had appeared over its doorway bearing the single word RESURGAM - I shall rise again!

Plymouth did rise again, though few who remembered the old town were happy with the new. Yet some old landmarks are still there. Locals meet at Derry's Cross as they always did. Sailors continue to throng Union Street on Saturday nights. Tourists still make a first stop at Plymouth Hoe to see the spot where Sir Francis Drake may or may not have played a famous game of bowls.

Within a bus journey of the city centre is some of the loveliest pastoral scenery in England. The South Hams is a wondrous collection of ancient towns, picturesque villages and spectacular coastal scenery, remaining fiercely independent of the great city not far away. The absence of major roads to the coast,

the inspiring walks and probably the mildest climate in mainland Britain, bring visitors back again and again. Caught between Plymouth and the Dart estuary in one direction and Dartmoor and the coast in the other, the South Hams have an identity and character all their own.

Its towns are modest in size and as old as town where officers from all over the world are trained. It has a long connection with the sea. Crusaders, privateers, naval armadas and D-Day invasion forces all set sail from here. Chaucer's 'shipman' from 'The Canterbury Tales', in reality John Hawley, one of England's greatest medieval merchants, lies buried in the church. The Dart estuary, surely

history. Kingsbridge is mostly Saxon in origin, though Iron Age man lived not far away. The twisting Kingsbridge estuary is reminiscent of the mysterious and muddy creeks of southern Cornwall, rather than anywhere else in Devon. Salcombe, the port at its mouth, seems to live for sailing, with a happy flotilla of yachts, dinghies and motor boats exploring the tidal waters on calm days.

Dartmouth, some miles east, climbs the steep hillside above its own estuary. This is a naval

Devon's most beautiful one, is navigable as far as Totnes, before it becomes a rushing watercourse winding up to Dartmoor. Agatha Christie lived on its banks at Greenway House, high above the ferry crossing at Dittisham, for many years.

Many consider that the stretch of coastline between Thurlestone and the Dart to be the finest in England. But it can be a cruel coast as well. Its high rocky cliffs have been the downfall of many ships, their wrecks littering the seabed just offshore. The coastline west of the Dart has sad recent memories. Several villages inland from Slapton Sands were evacuated during the Second World War, and the surrounding countryside was given over to the United States Army. Hundreds of young American soldiers and sailors died here and in Lyme Bay rehearsing for the D-Day landings. A stone obelisk and a recovered Sherman Tank near the great freshwater lake of Slapton Ley records their deeds and honours their sacrifice.

Now all is peaceful; the cry of the birds, the crash of the waves and the sough of the warm summer breeze have drowned out the horrendous noise of shot and shell. The South Hams too have 'risen again', managing to capture a peace and tranquillity perhaps more in keeping with Edwardian times than with the rush of a new Millennium.

DEVONPORT, THE ROYAL HOTEL 1890 22446
Devonport stands to the west of the city of Plymouth, and is the
newest of the three towns that make up Devon's largest urban
area. In Nelson's day the town was known simply as 'Dock' or
'Plymouth Dock', only acquiring its present name in 1824.

DEVONPORT, ROYAL MARINE BARRACKS 1890 22448
As a naval port, Plymouth has always had a large contingent of military personnel stationed around its various districts. Many impressive buildings, such as the barracks shown here, have been built to accommodate them.

DEVONPORT, TORPOINT FERRY BRIDGE 1890 22462
Torpoint is actually in Cornwall, and its ferry still makes regular journeys across the Tamar, taking workers across to Devonport Dockyard and the City of Plymouth. Before the construction of the Tamar suspension bridge, this was one of the few ways to cross the river.

DEVONPORT, MOUNT WISE 1890 22468

Below the fortifications of Mount Wise we can see a variety of shipping, from paddle steamers to ancient naval vessels, which were probably used as training depots. These seem to have more in common with Nelson's navy than with the iron-clad battleships that were starting to dock at Devonport at this time.

DEVONPORT, HALFPENNY BRIDGE 1904 52427

It is probable that Devonport abandoned its earlier name of Plymouth Dock as a gesture of independence. A huge community, both military and trading, grew around the naval yards with thousands of homes to cater for dockworkers and public houses in which to entertain shorebound sailors.

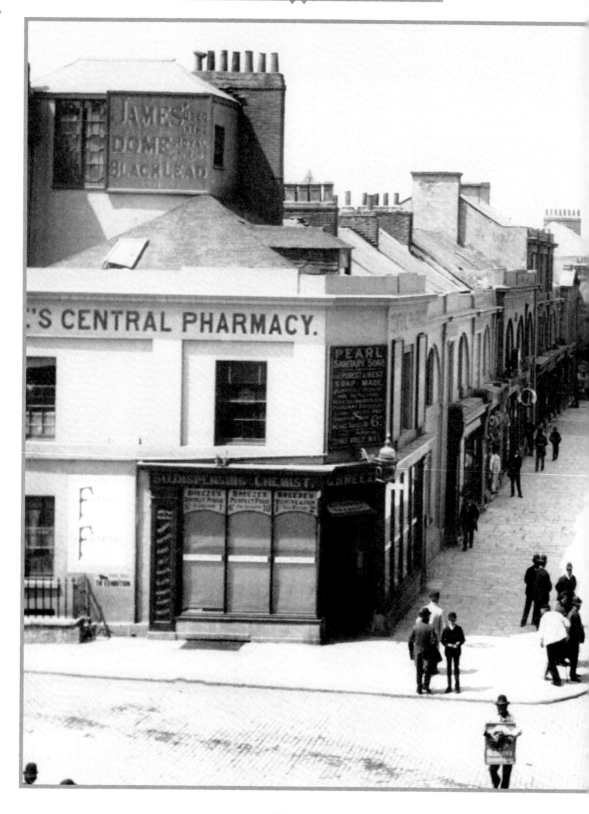

PLYMOUTH, THE GUILDHALL AND THE POST OFFICE 1889 22388

The City of Plymouth has given its name to some forty other Plymouths around the English-speaking world. The Pilgrim Fathers sailed from here in the early 17th century, landing near that part of America still known as Plymouth Rock.

PLYMOUTH, GEORGE STREET 1889 22397

Serving both a rural area round about, and hundreds of overseas ports by way of trade, Plymouth reached its mercantile heyday in Victorian times. For many years the Great Western Railway ended its journey at the city. Only with the construction of the Royal Albert Bridge across the Tamar to Saltash did the railway open up the Duchy of Cornwall.

PLYMOUTH, TAVISTOCK ROAD 1890 22423
The Tavistock road leads away from Plymouth to the fringes of Dartmoor, and has always been a busy highway. The supply of a great city in Victorian times called for the support of hundreds of local farmers, who would bring in endless amounts of food and other goods.

PLYMOUTH, THE BARBICAN 1890 22474
The Barbican lines Sutton Harbour, long a fishing quay and the original port of Plymouth. From here Elizabethan sailors, merchants and privateers would have set sail in search of profit and adventure on the high seas.

PLYMOUTH, THE CLOCK TOWER 1892 30597

One of the great tragedies in Plymouth's long history was the great air raids of the Second World War. Much of old Plymouth town was destroyed, irreplaceable old buildings were lost, and street patterns were changed with the rebuilding. Only through photographs and film can we see the Plymouth that these Victorians would have known. Ten thousand buildings were destroyed, and seventy thousand more damaged by the bombing.

PLYMOUTH, THE PIER 1898 41930
Plymouth never quite achieved the status of being a major seaside resort, though tourists have always bathed from its beaches and promenaded across the famous Hoe. The City's holiday value is as a touring centre. There are many delightful coves and coastal walks in the vicinity.

PLYMOUTH, THE LIDO AND WALKS 1934 86216
Below Plymouth Hoe, where legend tells us that Sir Francis Drake played that famous game of bowls, is a promenade for strolling or lounging on deckchairs. It is also an excellent viewpoint from which to watch ships entering and leaving Plymouth Sound.

PLYMOUTH
Onion Sellers 1907
A charming study of two young onion sellers taken by Frith during the long and prosperous 'Edwardian Afternoon'. Merchant ships brought goods from all over the world into Plymouth's harbours.

YEALMPTON
From the Bridge 1904
Yealmpton, always pronounced Yampton, stands on the River Yealm near to the end of its short journey from Dartmoor to the sea. The church is very much a Victorian restoration, but has some excellent old tombs, particularly the 17th-century one for Mary Copleston, whose effigy is surrounded by three of her seven children.

PLYMOUTH, ONION SELLERS 1907 59208

YEALMPTON, FROM THE BRIDGE 1904 52428

NEWTON FERRERS, BRIDGE END 1931 83975

Newton Ferrers and Noss Mayo, 'Newton and Noss' to all locals, line the opposite banks of the Yealm estuary. Both are delightful, with old Devon cob cottages and attractive gardens in an area of fine scenery. It is hard to imagine the crowded streets of Plymouth only a few miles away.

NOSS MAYO, RIVER YEALM 1901 46327

Noss Mayo's church, seen in the middle distance, was built on the orders of Lord Revelstoke in 1882 in a beautiful setting above both the village and river. The original parish church is now a picturesque ruin some distance away on the clifftops of Stoke Point.

BIGBURY-ON-SEA, FROM CLIMATON HILL 1924 76565
Bigbury-on-Sea lies on the shores of Bigbury Bay within site of Burgh Island, which may give the village its name. Many famous people such as Agatha Christie, who set novels in the locality, Noel Coward and Edward VIII stayed on Burgh Island and walked this wild coastline.

BIGBURY-ON-SEA, THE VILLAGE 1925 78342
Bigbury-on-Sea stands on a promontory above the River Avon, which rises high on southern Dartmoor. This was a rural backwater until well into the 20th century. It is interesting to see here the competition between horse and car as early as 1925. These two forms of transport still battle for space in the lanes of South Devon.

AVETON GIFFORD, THE CHURCH 1890 24534

AVETON GIFFORD
The Church 1890
Aveton Gifford (pronounced Auton, meaning the settlement on the Avon) stands at the head of the estuary. This fine church was destroyed in a 'tip-and-run' air raid in 1943 with considerable loss of life, but has since been sympathetically restored.

BANTHAM 1926
The tiny settlement of Bantham, with its passenger ferry and boat-houses, clings to the eastern bank of the Avon where the river makes one last sweeping curve before meeting the sea.

BANTHAM 1926 78324

THURLESTONE, THE VILLAGE 1918 68605

Thurlestone takes its name from a holed, or thirled, rock just out at sea in Bigbury Bay, which was mentioned in a Saxon charter way back in 845. Despite some garish modern buildings and the large golf course nearby, Thurlestone remains the attractive village we see here in 1918.

HOPE COVE, COTTAGES 1890 25260

Hope Cove was a simple fishing village cut off from the world until it was 'discovered' in the 20th century. It says a lot for its resilience that it has remained unspoiled, remaining a wonderful place to visit and to get away from the pressures of modern life.

HOPE COVE 1904 52467

Hope Cove remains one of the few safe anchorages between the Yealm estuary and Salcombe, several miles to the east. Tiny fishing smacks still set out from the cove each day, much as they probably did in 1588 when the Spanish Armada was first sighted off the Devon coast.

HOPE COVE 1925 78392

Much of this bare hillside between Outer and Inner Hope has now been built upon, but the tiny church remains and the coast nearby is wild and spectacular. Around the next headland is Ramillies Cove where HMS Ramillies was wrecked two centuries ago, with the loss of over 700 lives.

MALBOROUGH
Lower Town 1927

Malborough lies away from the coast, high above the Salcombe estuary, but it is an ideal place to stay when exploring the beautiful stretch of coastline between Bolt Head and Bolt Tail - the favourite scenery of many Devonians.

◆

SALCOMBE
The Quayside 1896

Salcombe is a small port at the mouth of the Kingsbridge estuary. It is so sheltered and mild that even oranges have been known to grow there. The town has become a haven for leisure yachtsmen, with many of its shops devoted to water sports and its old inns occupied by the sailing fraternity.

MALBOROUGH, LOWER TOWN 1927 79903

SALCOMBE, THE QUAYSIDE 1896 38483

SALCOMBE, GENERAL VIEW 1920 69808
Local tradition alleges that Alfred, Lord Tennyson wrote his famous poem 'Crossing the Bar' with the perilous entrance to the Salcombe estuary in mind. He certainly visited the town, though it has to be said that several other ports claim the honour of possessing the sand bar in question.

SALCOMBE, GULLET 1922 73255
A timeless scene in one of the many creeks of the long estuary that runs between Salcombe and Kingsbridge. The wooded banks of this stretch of water are best explored by boat at high tide, though even at low tide the extensive mud flats are home to a huge variety of birdlife.

SALCOMBE, FROM PORTLEMOUTH 1928 81014

A few ruined walls in the estuary mark the site of Fort Charles, which was garrisoned by the royalist army for four months in 1646 during the English Civil War. So bravely did they defend this hopeless position in the face of a mightier parliamentarian army that the Roundhead commander allowed them to leave with colours flying.

KINGSBRIDGE, THE BRIDGE 1890 24525

A bridge crossed the head of the Kingsbridge estuary as early as 962, though the surviving bridges in the area are medieval in origin. Notice the ghostly boat below the right-hand side of the bridge, evidence of the slow exposure of the photograph.

KINGSBRIDGE, TACKETT WOOD COTTAGES 1896 38428
Tackett or Ticket Wood is said to get its name from the nonconformists who worshipped here illegally centuries ago. Tradition suggests that tickets would be issued for these meetings by worshippers so as to avoid infiltration by spies, who might betray them to the authorities.

KINGSBRIDGE, FORE STREET 1896 38429
A steep hill leads away from the estuary to the top of Kingsbridge town. The settlement was probably established in Saxon times, though it did not become an important trading centre until the Abbot of Buckfast established a market here in 1219. Within a few years Kingsbridge and the adjoining manor of Dodbrooke achieved borough status.

KINGSBRIDGE, FORE STREET AND THE BANK 1896 38507

Fore Street boasts many excellent examples of Georgian and Victorian architecture, with a Shambles and market arcade rebuilt in 1796. Its grammar school was founded in 1670 by Thomas Crispin - a sign of the importance of this growing community.

KINGSBRIDGE, FORE STREET 1896 38510

One local resident had a cynical sense of humour. His epitaph in the parish church runs: 'Here lie I at the chancel door; Here lie I because I'm poor; The farther in the more you'll pay; Here lie I as warm as they'.

KINGSBRIDGE, THE RIVER 1920 69826
Legend relates that a Saxon king, on a progress through his realm, wondered how he could cross a creek without getting his feet wet. An obliging servant stepped into the water offering to piggy-back the king across - hence Kingsbridge.

KINGSBRIDGE, THE RIVER 1920 69824
Kingsbridge church, seen here in the distance, is dedicated to St Edmund the Martyr, an unusual dedication for a Devon church. Its worshippers must have seen a great variety of ships and boats use the estuary far below.

FROGMORE, THE VILLAGE 1904 52461
Frogmore Creek makes an eastward journey from the Kingsbridge estuary, narrowing by the medieval road bridge. In the nearby Geese Quarries finely bedded slate was worked for use in local church building. Some of the quarry's workers would probably have lived in these cottages.

TORCROSS, THE SANDS 1896 38438
During the Second World War villagers were evacuated from many villages around the South Hams so that the district could become a D-Day training ground for American troops, who would practise landings on Slapton Sands. More Americans died training here than were killed on Utah Beach on D-Day.

SLAPTON, THE POST OFFICE 1925 78245
Slapton was one of the villages evacuated during the war. Villagers were given only a few days to pack up their belongings and move away. Many buildings were damaged during the exercises but now, happily, show few scars. An obelisk, a gift from the United States Army, can be seen on the nearby sands, its plaque thanking the villagers for their sacrifice.

STRETE, THE VILLAGE 1925 78256
Strete stands on the winding lanes which form the highway between Dartmouth and the villages clustered around the great freshwater lake of Slapton Ley. Strete's main road is seldom now as peaceful and car-free as it was in the 1920s. There are some delightful walks in the area, and it is a pity so many motorists do not take the time to halt and explore.

STRETE, HILLSIDE AND FROGWELL 1925 78255
Two walkers enjoy the country lanes of the South Hams in the days before the highway was dominated by motor cars. There is an extensive network of footpaths and bridleways in this area, and ramblers and riders can still see unspoiled scenes if they care to wander away from the roads.

DARTMOUTH, DARTMOUTH REGATTA 1889 21648
Queen Victoria much admired the town of Dartmouth and its beautiful estuary, recording in her journal that '...the place is lovely, with its wooded rocks and church and castle at the entrance. It puts me so much in mind of the beautiful Rhine...'

DARTMOUTH, THE ROYAL NAVAL COLLEGE 1918 68612A
Generations of naval officers have trained in this impressive building, or on the old ships moored here in the days
before the land base was established. It was here that Princess Elizabeth, later Queen Elizabeth II, first met her hus-
band Prince Phillip.

DARTMOUTH, DITTISHAM ON THE DART 1889 21617
Dittisham is one of the larger villages along the steeply wooded banks of the romantic Dart estuary. A foot ferry
takes passengers across the river to Greenway, once the home of Dame Agatha Christie.

Torbay and Teignbridge

IN ADMIRAL NELSON's day it was said that the entire British naval fleet could take shelter in Torbay during stormy weather. On calmer days the bay was used as a supply depot for ships participating in the blockade of France during the Napoleonic Wars. Among the first visitors to the area were the wives and families of serving officers, who took up residence in Torquay so as to be near their loved ones.

Napoleon Bonaparte must have appreciated Torbay's strategic importance as he paced the decks of HMS Bellerophon: it lay anchored off Torquay before the deposed Emperor was shipped to his last exile on St Helena. Napoleon, basking in the interest of the crowds who came out by boat to catch a glimpse of him, famously compared the bay to the best parts of Italy and Elba.

The bay's three major resorts are all very different from each other in character. Brixham remains a charming old fishing town, beloved of artists, photographers and the tourists who throng the quay in the summer to watch the trawlers come and go. It is the most unspoiled of the towns, and glories in its rugged and romantic setting. Paignton, in contrast, is a happy family resort, with two miles of safe bathing on golden sandy beaches. The Singer family's residence in Paignton, and the construction of the imposing Oldway Mansion, raised the profile of the resort across the country, and the tourists flooded in.

If you look down from one of its many hilltops, Torquay gives the impression of having grown out of the twisted limestone on which it rests, its elegant buildings clinging to the peaks, slopes and hollows of a wild and broken landscape. If it has not always succeeded in its aim to be an upmarket watering place, it has at least weathered the vagaries of the 20th century with some considerable flair and dignity. A walk around its steep and winding streets reveals much about both the social history of holiday resorts and the longer story of those who worked the land before the tourists arrived. Its chosen title, 'Queen of the English Riviera', is deserved, for much of the old town exudes a regal charm.

A walk or sail eastwards brings the traveller to the estuaries of the Teign and the Exe. The land between is Teignbridge, though the name is a political rather a geographical delineation. At its heart is the market town of

Newton Abbot - the focus for shoppers throughout the district. This community was old even before 1688 when William of Orange marched through on his journey to the British throne; it was an ancient monastic holding, as its name implies.

Following the Teign estuary downstream brings us to Teignmouth, Devon's second oldest holiday resort and still a popular place for day-trippers. This old settlement has been battered by history, for almost every enemy of England throughout the last two millennia seems to have raided and burnt it down. Unkind planners in the last century have not always done their best by Teignmouth, but somehow it has survived; the fact that its best parts remain so little changed since these photographs were taken says a great deal for its durability.

Dawlish is a delight, a charming regency town, with Brunel's railway running along its sea-front in what must surely be one of the most picturesque journeys in England. Black swans cadge food as they swim up and down the Dawlish Water, that charming brook dividing the town, and summer bathers enjoy the mile of sand that runs to Dawlish Warren.

Torbay and Teignbridge are the most urbanised and crowded sections of the South Devon coast, and their delights are not always as obvious as those on the wilder coastlines of East Devon or the South Hams. But a little exploration reveals much about the character and development of this part of the county, and a great deal about the evolution of the English seaside resort.

BRIXHAM, INNER HARBOUR 1889 21552
Despite its fame as a fishing port from the Middle Ages onwards, people have lived around Brixham for some half a million years. Caves under the limestone cliffs were occupied from the early Stone Age. Iron Age dwellers built a fortification on Berry Head, and Celtic inhabitants would have collected salt and fish where the harbour now stands.

BRIXHAM, FISHING BOATS 1889 21558
This idyllic picture of the Brixham fishing fleet gives some idea of just how much the fishing industry dominated the town for hundreds of years. At the height of the Victorian age some 200 trawlers would regularly put to sea from Brixham harbour.

BRIXHAM, THE PRINCE OF ORANGE MONUMENT 1891 28241

William of Orange, whose statue looks away from the sea and towards England, landed at Brixham on 5 November 1688 to depose the Catholic King James II and to herald 'a glorious revolution'. William and his Dutch troops received a hearty welcome from local families.

BRIXHAM, GENERAL VIEW 1896 38882

The fishermen of Brixham refined the technique of trawling for their catch close to the bottom of the sea; this technique mostly replaced the earlier drifting. The sailing trawlers needed to work with the tide and a stiff wind - up to force six or seven - behind them if the nets were to be trawled successfully.

BRIXHAM, INNER HARBOUR 1906 54039

After the 1850s the new railway from Churston meant that Brixham fish could be sent swiftly to towns and cities throughout Britain. Most Brixham trawlers were owned by shareholders, with family and friends holding shares. Brixham enjoyed a prosperity rarely seen during the hard times of Victorian England.

BRIXHAM, FORE STREET 1922 73032
For many years Brixham's Fore Street was the principal thoroughfare between Higher Brixham and the harbour. Here we see it at a time when the shops catered mostly for local fishing families. Notice the horse-drawn cart and the absence of much other traffic.

BRIXHAM, BOLTON CROSS 1922 73033
This view shows Bolton Cross on the road to Higher Brixham before it became the traffic-packed road junction it is today. Local people always referred to Lower Brixham as 'Fish Town' and Higher Brixham as 'Cow Town' after their respective industries of fishing and farming.

BRIXHAM, THE PARISH CHURCH 1922 73048
St Mary's, the parish church of Higher Brixham, was the town's original place of worship, dating back to the 15th century. There are some impressive altar tombs and a font dating back to the 1300s. This lovely church tends to be missed by visitors, who speed by to see the Rev. Lyte's new church of All Saints', standing so prominently above the harbour.

BRIXHAM, THE HARBOUR 1925 78489
All Saints' Church contains a memorial to the Reverend Lyte, author of 'Abide With Me' and 'Praise My Soul, the King of Heaven'. Lyte was the much loved Victorian parson of the fishing town, living high above the town at Berry Head House.

BRIXHAM, THE HARBOUR 1925 78490
Brixham has known sadness and tragedy as well as the tough but idyllic life of the fishing heyday. Two hundred Brixham men died during the First World War, many of them fishermen. This led to a declining fishing industry and an idle fleet during the depression of the 1920s.

BRIXHAM, THE HARBOUR 1925 78492
Until the 20th century, shipbuilding was Brixham's most important industry after fishing. Small merchant vessels and privateers were constructed during earlier times for trade and piracy, though in later years many of the ship-builders concentrated on building and repairing fishing boats.

PAIGNTON, THE PIER 1889 21529

Paignton pier, one of the oldest in Britain, strides 800 feet out to sea; we see it here in all its Victorian finery. Of all the Torbay resorts, only Paignton has a pier, owing to a combination of its popularity as a family resort and the gently sloping sands that facilitated the pier's construction.

PAIGNTON, THE HARBOUR 1890 25907

Paignton's harbour is an extension of a simple early shelter for shipping. Though not as protected as the harbour at Brixham, it maintained a fishing fleet for several centuries. It is used today mostly for leisure boating.

PAIGNTON, THE BATHING BEACH 1896 38545
Paignton's beaches and coves give a combined sea-frontage of over two miles; this led to the growth of the town's satellite villages of Preston and Goodrington. These long stretches of sand enjoy the safest bathing in Torbay.

PAIGNTON, THE PROMENADE AND SANDS 1907 58415A
Paignton became fashionable with the arrival of the Singer family, who built Oldway Mansion in 1874. The sewing machine millionaires completed their home in 1907, inspired by the architectural wonders of Versailles. The cream of Victorian society visited the Singers at their imposing seaside home.

PAIGNTON, CHURCH STREET 1912 64719
St John's Church originally dated from the 12th century, but was rebuilt three hundred years later. It is said to stand on the site of a Bronze Age burial mound. The Kirkham chapel within contains the tombs of Sir William Kirkham and his wife, who died in the 17th century.

PAIGNTON, PRESTON SANDS 1918 68533
This photograph shows a Torbay at war. Seaplanes from the newly-formed Royal Air Force are pulled up on the beach - perhaps being used either for recruitment or anti-submarine duties. There is a marked absence of young men - all away at the Front.

PAIGNTON
The Harbour 1922
By the 1920s the harbour was used almost entirely by small-scale fishermen and pleasure craft. Here we see their nets and lobster pots, though some had begun to diversify into pleasure trips for tourists as a supplement to their incomes.

TORQUAY
Cockington 1901
The picture-postcard village of Cockington forms a green oasis between the urban sprawls of Paignton and Torquay. The thatched building on the left is the famous Cockington Forge.

PAIGNTON, THE HARBOUR 1922 73067

TORQUAY, COCKINGTON 1901 47821

COCKINGTON, COURT COTTAGE 1889 21541
Despite the throng of tourists on summer afternoons, Cockington retains its old-world charm with its picturesque thatched cottages, bee-haunted gardens, lovely old church and modest stately home.

TORQUAY, BEACON TERRACE 1888 21428
Before the coming of tourism, Torquay was an obscure fishing hamlet, its villagers scratching a living from the sea, smuggling and lime burning. All of these activities continued well into the Victorian age.

TORQUAY, THE HARBOUR 1890 25921

St John's Church, situated dramatically above Torquay harbour, was built in limestone excavated from its own site by G E Street in 1861. Its west window was designed by the pre-Raphaelite artist Edward Burne-Jones. The church is supposedly haunted by the ghosts of two former organists, whose music can still be heard echoing over the town.

TORQUAY, ABBEY CRESCENT 1896 38598

The elegant Abbey Crescent was built in 1858 in anticipation of the opening of the nearby railway station the following year. Its designers considered that this new access to Torquay would popularise this hitherto quiet end of town.

TORQUAY, FROM VANE HILL 1901 47806
An early visitor said of Torquay: 'It is not England, but a bit of sunny Italy taken bodily from its rugged coast and placed here amid the green places and the pleasant pastoral lanes of beautiful Devon'.

TORQUAY, THE STRAND 1906 54015
Apart from a considerable increase in traffic, Torquay's Strand has changed very little since this photograph was taken in Edwardian times. The harbour was at that time still the preserve of local fishermen, but today the area is monopolised by pleasure craft and luxury yachts.

TORQUAY, THE FARM 1906 54016

Until recently, when Torbay succumbed to urban sprawl, the green fields of Devon did come almost to the heart of the town. Only to the north of Torquay and around Cockington can scenes such as this be easily found.

TORQUAY, VANE HILL 1920 69574

Above Torquay harbour stands Vane Hill, seen here from the Rock Walk. It was named after the prominent weathervane placed here early in the 19th century by Mrs Johnes, a local benefactor who spent a great deal of her own money on improving the growing town.

TORQUAY, PRINCESS PARADE 1920 69579
In the 1920s Torquay became not only a venue for family holidays but a much-loved destination for day trips, with tourists arriving by train and charabanc. Torquay had been a popular escape from the horrors of the Great War, and many ex-servicemen returned in the years of peace.

TORQUAY, THE STRAND 1920 69586
Air raids in the Second World War led to the decline in Torquay harbour's use as a commercial port, though ferries have continued to ply their trade to the Channel Islands from here. The harbour marina is now full of luxury yachts.

TORQUAY, ABBEY SANDS 1924 76401
On a crowded summer's day, sunbathers enjoy the warmth on Abbey sands. Modesty dictated that bathers should get changed in one of the long line of changing tents.

TORQUAY, THE HARBOUR 1928 81106
Beyond Torquay harbour is the fine sweep of Torbay. In Nelson's day the entire British fleet could anchor within the sheltering arms of the bay. Napoleon Bonaparte, a prisoner on HMS Bellerophon after Waterloo, compared the scenery to Elba and Italy.

TORQUAY, ANSTEY'S COVE 1896 38609
One of a number of attractive coves on the length of coastline between Torquay and Babbacombe, Anstey's Cove has been a favourite retreat for holidaymakers since Victorian times, when the proprietor would provide cream teas and swimming lessons for patrons.

BABBACOMBE, THE DOWNS 1918 68547
Before the development of Babbacombe as a small holiday resort, its isolated coves were used by smugglers such as Bob Elliott of Brixham and Jack Rattenbury of Beer. The present coastal footpath came into being as a patrol route for the coastguards who had the duty of intercepting illicit cargoes.

TORQUAY, BABBACOMBE BAY 1924 76437
Babbacombe's beaches were popular with early visitors to the resort, such as Oscar Wilde and Edward VII. Boats would convey tourists from the busier resorts to Babbacombe's landing stage, so that they might indulge in bathing and picnicking.

ODDICOMBE BEACH 1889 21491
Early visitors faced a long climb to Babbacombe after a day on the beaches, but in the 1920s a cliff railway - still in use today - was built, making the journey much easier.

BABBACOMBE, THE BEACH 1925 78445
Several winding walks form an alternative way to return to Babbacombe for the energetic, or in the winter months when the cliff railway is closed. There are superb views across Lyme Bay from the clifftops, and Portland Bill can be seen on a clear day.

NEWTON ABBOT, THE CLOCK TOWER 1898 42492
Newton Abbot and Newton Bushel were two discrete settlements at the head of the Teign estuary when William of Orange arrived there from Brixham in 1688, on his way to displace James II as King of England.

NEWTON ABBOT, FROM DECOY 1906 56571

The site of the town was granted to the monks of Torre Abbey by William de Briwere in 1196, hence the second part of the name. As the town grew it spread rapidly across the parishes of Wolborough, Highweek and Newton Bushel, forming the conurbation we see today.

NEWTON ABBOT, ST LEONARD'S TOWER 1906 56572

St Leonard's Tower is all that remains of a 14th-century church demolished in 1836. It now forms a centrepiece to this busy market town, familiar to the many local people who come to shop each week from dozens of surrounding towns and villages.

NEWTON ABBOT, THE MARKET 1925 78550
Newton Abbot market has changed a great deal in both character and appearance since this photograph was taken in the 1920s. But farmers from all over South Devon still bring their animals to the town for the Wednesday livestock sales.

NEWTON ABBOT, COURTENAY STREET 1906 56574
Much of Victorian Newton Abbot was constructed under the watchful eyes of the influential local Courtenay family who owned much of the land. Courtenay Street and Courtenay Park are named in their honour.

NEWTON ABBOT, COURTENAY PARK 1906 56576
An Edwardian lady, parasol folded in hand, shelters in the shade of the trees at the entrance to Courtenay Park. The town's wealthier residents lived in sumptuous villas at this end of Newton Abbot.

SHALDON
Fore Street 1922
Shaldon remains an unspoiled regency fishing village on the Torquay side of the Teign estuary. A long bridge and foot-ferry lead across to neighbouring Teignmouth. The stretch of water between and Shaldon's sandy beaches are crammed with boats of every description.

TEIGNMOUTH
From Torquay Road 1890
Teignmouth is the second-oldest seaside resort in Devon; it has attracted visitors from the middle of the 18th century. It is seen here from the hillside above Shaldon across the broad sweep of the Teign estuary.

SHALDON, FORE STREET 1922 73108A

TEIGNMOUTH, FROM TORQUAY ROAD 1890 26021

TEIGNMOUTH, THE PARADE 1903 49559
Teignmouth remained a fashionable resort for two
centuries, particularly during the Napoleonic Wars
when eminent socialites made the town their own.
Early visitors included Jane Austen, John Keats and
Admiral Sir Edward Pellew.

TEIGNMOUTH, FROM THE PIER 1903 49560
Teignmouth was not always the peaceful holiday resort
we see here. The early Saxon town was attacked several times by Danish raiders, was destroyed by the
French in 1340 and 1690, and badly bombed during
the Second World War.

TEIGNMOUTH
The Terrace Walk 1911
The sea wall leads to the Parson and Clerk rocks, with the railway - surely one of the loveliest stretches of line in the country - running alongside. On stormy days the sea washes over both this path and the speeding trains.

TEIGNMOUTH
Whale Bones 1922
These whale bones were brought to the town by a local trader, a reminder of Teignmouth's importance as a port. Local ships would sail regularly across the Atlantic, bound for Newfoundland and other American destinations. The whale bones are no longer in position.

TEIGNMOUTH, THE TERRACE WALK 1911 63698

TEIGNMOUTH, WHALE BONES 1922 73089

DAWLISH, THE SEAFRONT FROM THE ROYAL HOTEL 1890 26059
A place familiar to all train travellers through Devon, Dawlish nestles across the sides of a broad combe, with the railway line protecting the town from the sea. The resort gets its name from the dark stream, doflisc in Anglo-Saxon, which now runs through the resort's central parkland.

DAWLISH, THE BLENHEIM HOTEL 1925 78435
Dawlish began as two discrete hamlets, one inland by the parish church and another on the seashore, but quickly grew as the first visitors arrived to holiday in the late 18th century. Few concessions were made to this new source of income until well into the next century.

DAWLISH, THE BEACH 1922 72990
Like Teignmouth and Lyme Regis, Dawlish was much-loved by fashionable society during the 19th century. Jane Austen visited the town and mentioned it in one of her novels, while Charles Dickens chose it as the birthplace of his eponymous hero in 'Nicholas Nickleby'.

DAWLISH, BOAT COVE 1925 78437

The coves around Dawlish and Teignmouth were used extensively by smugglers until Isambard Kingdom Brunel built his atmospheric railway line and the accompanying cliff tunnels in the first half of the 19th century, making the landing of cargoes more difficult.

DAWLISH, THE LAWNS 1925 78441

After 1803 the environs of the Dawlish Water were landscaped to provide the kind of pleasure grounds expected in fashionable resorts of this period. Today the stream is a haven for wildlife, including Dawlish's famous black swans.

DAWLISH, DAWLISH WATER 1928 81171
The Dawlish Water and its high tributary the Smallacombe Brook rise on the wooded heathland of Little Haldon Hill, which rises eight hundred feet at the back of the town. Walking the length of the Water was a favourite excursion for early visitors, and can still be enjoyed today.

DAWLISH, KINGS PARADE 1903 49583
Brunel, showing considerable foresight, did not cut Dawlish off from the sea when he built his railway, but incorporated its walls into a splendid promenade which can be followed all the way to Dawlish Warren on calm days.

DAWLISH WARREN
Mount Pleasant 1906

Mount Pleasant Inn still stands above the marshlands of Dawlish Warren, though it has changed somewhat since this photograph was taken. Two hundred years ago it was the headquarters of a notorious smuggling gang, who would store their contraband in the tunnels and cellars beneath the building. One longer tunnel is said to have run down to the beach.

◆

EXMINSTER
Turf Lock 1906

The old Turf Lock Inn stands near the lock gates where the Exeter Canal - probably the oldest in England - meets the Exe estuary. This popular public house can be reached only by boat, bicycle or on foot - cars are not allowed on the narrow track across Exminster marshes.

DAWLISH WARREN, MOUNT PLEASANT 1906 54054

EXMINSTER, TURF LOCK 1906 53983

THE EAST DEVON COAST

THE EXE ESTUARY, a paradise for birdwatchers, forms a formidable barrier between Teignbridge and East Devon. And perhaps it is just as well, for both the geography and character of this next stretch of coastline are very different from anything we have seen so far. Even its resort towns - Exmouth, Budleigh Salterton, and Sidmouth - have a sedate, old-fashioned feel that the Torbay resorts have probably lost for ever.

This is not surprising, given that Exmouth is the oldest watering place in Devon. Seaside holidays were almost invented there, and even with its present massive influx of holidaymakers, it has managed to retain the air of dignity it probably enjoyed during the Regency, when Lady Byron and Lady Nelson were typical of the illustrious guests who enjoyed its varied delights.

A little further along the coast, where the tide plays fitfully with its beach of large round stones, or 'pobbles', is Budleigh Salterton, often unfairly labelled as a seaside retirement home for aged colonels; here, you might expect to see Noel Coward or Miss Marple pacing the streets. The label is an unkind and rather hoary local joke, for the folk are friend-ly and younger than you might imagine, even if the town itself seems to be a habitation by the sea rather than anything like a traditional holiday resort. But with the delightful coastal scenery and the placid waters of the River Otter to explore, who needs artificial entertainments anyway?

Sidmouth occupies a broad green valley where the long line of red sandstone cliffs breaks to admit the departure of the tiny River Sid. Queen Victoria spent some of her childhood here in the company of her impoverished parents, and always held the town in high regard. It is as good a centre as anywhere else to explore the wild and unspoiled hinterland of East Devon, with its coastal footpaths and long stretches of lonely heathland.

Between the resorts are miles of secluded and dramatic coastline, broken occasionally by old smuggling villages such as Branscombe and Beer. Even as late as the 19th century Jack Rattenbury, the 'Rob Roy of the West', ran the landings of night cargo hereabouts, surviving to gain a pension, write a book of memoirs, and pass away more peacefully than some of his fellows. His contemporary Ambrose Stapleton was the parson of East Budleigh, but the ringleader of a smuggling gang for all that. Over at Sidmouth the entire tribe of the Mutter family seemed to have dabbled with the illicit trade. Many a villager in East Devon must have 'watched the wall, my darling' while the gentlemen went by. Contraband was hidden in the tombs of Branscombe churchyard; one unfortunate customs officer lies there as well, having 'slipped' over a cliff. As far as the landscape goes, little has really changed since those hard but romantic days.

As the red cliffs turn to white chalk on the journey eastwards, the coastline dips past the towns of Seaton and Axmouth, where the wind blows through the reeds of the silted Axe estuary. Beyond is the great landslip where hundreds of acres of cliff tumbled into the sea early in the 19th century. Here East Devon merges imperceptibly with West Dorset, and our long journey along the county's southern coast comes to an end.

TOPSHAM, THE STRAND 1906 53993
Topsham, at the head of the Exe estuary, became a seaport of considerable importance in the Middle Ages. Trade with Holland led to the building of many of the Dutch-style gabled houses that line the Strand.

TOPSHAM, THE QUAY 1906 53990
The Exe estuary around Topsham is one of the finest places in Britain for birdwatching. Regular cruises take enthusiasts down-river to see the famous avocets on the river's mud banks. These fisherfolk and boatmen share a rare idle moment in a busy day.

LYMPSTONE 1896 37645

Lympstone, an artists' paradise, commands beautiful views over the Exe estuary with its wonderful birdlife. Notice the fishing nets - and the fishermen's trousers - hanging up to dry.

EXMOUTH, THE SANDS 1890 26261

At the beginning of the last millennium, marauding Danes landed on these sandy beaches and put the village of Exmouth to fire and sword. But the settlement rose from the ashes; in the year 1347 it was wealthy enough to contribute ten vessels to attack Calais. Its maritime activities continue to this day.

EXMOUTH, ROLLE STREET 1895 36055
Exmouth prospered as a holiday resort - the first in Devon - from the early 18th century, coming into its own when the Continent was closed to visitors during the Napoleonic Wars. Rolle Street was named after the prominent family that lived at nearby Bicton House.

EXMOUTH, THE PIER 1896 37624
Exmouth is still a busy little port, though merchant vessels are now outnumbered by sailing boats. A ferry crosses the Exe from here to the village of Starcross on the opposite bank.

EXMOUTH, VIEW FROM THE BEACON 1925 78594

Exmouth's long sea front and sandy beaches made sea-bathing a popular recreation from the town's earliest days as a resort. Tourists came for the bracing air and social activities. Some, such as Lady Nelson, widow of the Admiral, never left. She lies buried in the churchyard at nearby Littleham.

BUDLEIGH SALTERTON, THE PROMENADE 1898 42448

Budleigh Salterton stands to the west of the silted estuary of the River Otter. Its own beach is sandless and full of large pebbles, which seem to sing as the tides play across them. It gets its name from the salterns, or salt pans, used by the monks of nearby Otterton Priory.

BUDLEIGH SALTERTON, HIGH STREET 1898 42453
One early visitor to Budleigh was the Pre-Raphaelite artist Sir John Everett Millais, who lived for some time at The Octagon at the western end of the parade. His famous painting 'The Boyhood of Raleigh' features the sea wall across the road from where Millais stayed.

BUDLEIGH SALTERTON, HIGH STREET 1918 68726
The sheltered town soon acquired a reputation as a retirement haven and resort for the more sedate visitor. There are excellent walks in the vicinity, not only along the coastal footpath but also across the wilds of Woodbury Common.

EAST BUDLEIGH, THE VILLAGE 1938 88621
This attractive village at the lower end of the Vale of the Otter was the birthplace in 1552 of Sir Walter Raleigh. The Raleigh family home, Hayes Barton, can still be seen in all its Elizabethan splendour a mile from the village. There are reminders of the Raleigh family in St Michael's parish church.

EAST BUDLEIGH, THE VILLAGE 1938 88622
Two other famous residents of East Budleigh were two smuggling parsons - Matthew Mundy and Ambrose Stapleton. Both clerical gentlemen led the local smuggling gangs, hiding the contraband in the old vicarage - now a beautiful thatched house called Vicars Mead.

OTTERTON, THE VILLAGE 1906 56671

OTTERTON
The Village 1906
A little further upstream along the Otter is Otterton. Originally granted to the monks of St Michel in Normandy, Otterton's priory remained an important religious house until Henry VIII's dissolution of the monasteries.

◆

SIDMOUTH
High Street 1906
Sidmouth began as a small fishing town with a bustling local market, but even these activities had begun to decline by the time the first visitors arrived in the late 18th century. As with many similar resorts, the Napoleonic Wars boosted Sidmouth's fortunes, with so many people being forced to holiday at home.

SIDMOUTH, HIGH STREET 1906 53807

SIDMOUTH
The Esplanade 1918

Sidmouth's sea wall was first built in the 1830s, though attempts to create a satisfactory harbour failed. Fashionable hotels soon lined the front, with villa residences and smart cottages being erected along the slopes of Sid Vale to cater for a dramatic increase in the resident population.

◆

SIDMOUTH
Looking West 1924

In the early years of the 19th century the impoverished Duke of Kent came to live at Woolbrook Glen. He died at the house in 1820, though not before he had taken his baby daughter in his arms to see the sea, boasting to locals 'one day she will be your queen'. Many years later, Queen Victoria placed a window in the parish church as a monument to the father who had loved her so much.

SIDMOUTH, THE ESPLANADE 1918 68739

SIDMOUTH, LOOKING WEST 1924 76360

SIDMOUTH, THE ESPLANADE AND THE BEACH 1934 86238

In the 1930s Sidmouth acquired a reputation as an upmarket holiday resort, not so much for its sea-bathing as for the tranquillity of its setting and the mildness of its climate. In the distance we see the great cliff of High Peak - one of the highest points along the Devon coast.

BRANSCOMBE, YE OLD MASON'S ARMS 1931 84115

Branscombe is strung out down a deep valley running from the Devon downlands to the sea at Branscombe Mouth. Its ancient church, working smithy and popular inn brings its admirers back again and again. Few villages in England enjoy such a beautiful setting.

BEER, THE VILLAGE 1892 31318

Beer was the birthplace in 1788 of the smuggler Jack Rattenbury, who lived a life of adventure landing untaxed cargoes along much of the Devon coast. The old rogue lived to a respectable, though gout-ridden, old age, writing his memoirs and receiving a small pension from the respectable local worthy Lord Rolle, who admired the wily Jack's nerve - and may have received a keg of brandy in return.

BEER, THE BEACH 1898 42434

BEER
The Beach 1898
Local tradition says that a Spanish galleon was wrecked in the cove here during the 17th century, soon after the village had been depopulated by a plague. The crew, it is said, settled down at Beer, married the local womenfolk and repopulated the community.

BEER
Pillow Lace Workers 1901
Lace-making has always been an important tradition in East Devon, though it would be a rare sight today to see it carried out in the street by a local cottager. The lace for Queen Victoria's wedding dress was made in Beer at a cost of £1000.

BEER, PILLOW LACE WORKERS 1901 47861

BEER, EAST CLIFF 1907 58071
Beer stone has been quarried for centuries and used in important buildings across England. To the west of the village is a labyrinth of man-made caverns from which the stone for Exeter Cathedral was taken. The Quarry Caves are now an exciting tourist attraction.

BEER, FISHING BOATS 1918 68702
This picturesque locality has always attracted the eye of artist and photographer. One Victorian guide book writer described Beer as 'a rare subject for the pencil'. The notable Victorian artist Hamilton Macallum settled in Beer, and exhibited many local scenes at the Royal Academy in London. A memorial to him can be found just above the beach.

BEER, THE VILLAGE 1922 72943
Beer is not in any sense a holiday resort, though many cottages are to let and there are caravan parks nearby.
However, many visitors love the charm of this fishing village with its unspoiled beach, pleasant inns and occasional antique fairs.

SEATON, WHITE CLIFF FROM THE BEACH 1898 42425
The strange colours, white and red, of the cliffs around Seaton give a striking effect when the sun falls upon them.
They are notoriously crumbly, and rock falls are common.

SEATON, FORE STREET 1895 36081

Seaton is a mostly Victorian town hard by the mouth of the River Axe. Though never one of Devon's more fashionable resorts, it has a charm of its own and an attractive setting. Its close proximity to the Dorset border makes it an ideal place to stay for anyone exploring both counties.

AXMOUTH, THE VILLAGE 1927 79802

The end of our coastal journey brings us to one of the finest churches in Devon. St Michael's is a delight. Originally early Norman, it was altered and enlarged in 1330, and a perpendicular tower was added in the 15th century. Axmouth, the last coastal community wholly in Devon, was an important port until its river entrance silted up.

Index

FRITH PRODUCTS & SERVICES

Francis Frith would doubtless be pleased to know that the pioneering publishing venture he started in 1860 still continues today. Over a hundred and forty years later, The Francis Frith Collection continues in the same innovative tradition and is now one of the foremost publishers of vintage photographs in the world. Some of the current activities include:

INTERIOR DECORATION

Today Frith's photographs can be seen framed and as giant wall murals in thousands of pubs, restaurants, hotels, banks, retail stores and other public buildings throughout the country. In every case they enhance the unique local atmosphere of the places they depict and provide reminders of gentler days in an increasingly busy and frenetic world.

PRODUCT PROMOTIONS

Frith products are used by many major companies to promote the sales of their own products or to reinforce their own history and heritage. Frith promotions have been used by Hovis bread, Courage beers, Scots Porage Oats, Colman's mustard, Cadbury's foods, Mellow Birds coffee, Dunhill pipe tobacco, Guinness, and Bulmer's Cider.

GENEALOGY AND FAMILY HISTORY

As the interest in family history and roots grows world-wide, more and more people are turning to Frith's photographs of Great Britain for images of the towns, villages and streets where their ancestors lived; and, of course, photographs of the churches and chapels where their ancestors were christened, married and buried are an essential part of every genealogy tree and family album.

FRITH PRODUCTS

All Frith photographs are available Framed or just as Mounted Prints and Posters (size 23 x 16 inches). These may be ordered from the address below. Other products available are - Address Books, Calendars, Jigsaws, Canvas Prints, Postcards and local and prestige books.

THE INTERNET

Already ninety thousand Frith photographs can be viewed and purchased on the internet through the Frith websites and a myriad of partner sites.

For more detailed information on Frith products, look at this site:
www.francisfrith.com

See the complete list of Frith Books at: www.francisfrith.com
This web site is regularly updated with the latest list of publications from The Francis Frith Collection. If you wish to buy books relating to another part of the country that your local bookshop does not stock, you may purchase on-line.

For further information, trade, or author enquiries please contact us at the address below:
The Francis Frith Collection, Unit 6, Oakley Business Park, Wylye Road, Dinton, Wiltshire SP3 5EU.
Tel: +44 (0)1722 716 376 Fax: +44 (0)1722 716 881 Email: sales@francisfrith.co.uk

---

See Frith products on the internet at www.francisfrith.com

FREE PRINT OF YOUR CHOICE
CHOOSE A PHOTOGRAPH FROM THIS BOOK
+ £3.80 POSTAGE

Mounted Print
Overall size 14 x 11 inches (355 x 280mm)

TO RECEIVE YOUR FREE PRINT

Choose any Frith photograph in this book

Simply complete the Voucher opposite and return it with your remittance for £3.50 (to cover postage and handling) and we will print the photograph of your choice in SEPIA (size 11 x 8 inches) and supply it in a cream mount ready to frame (overall size 14 x 11 inches).

Order additional Mounted Prints
at HALF PRICE - £12.00 each (normally £24.00)

If you would like to order more Frith prints from this book, possibly as gifts for friends and family, you can buy them at half price (with no additional postage costs).

Have your Mounted Prints framed

For an extra £20.00 per print you can have your mounted print(s) framed in an elegant polished wood and gilt moulding, overall size 16 x 13 inches (no additional postage required).

IMPORTANT!

❶ Please note: aerial photographs and photographs with a reference number starting with a "Z" are not Frith photographs and cannot be supplied under this offer.

❷ Offer valid for delivery to one UK address only.

❸ These special prices are only available if you use this form to order. You must use the ORIGINAL VOUCHER on this page (no copies permitted). We can only despatch to one UK address.

❹ This offer cannot be combined with any other offer.

As a customer your name & address will be stored by Frith but not sold or rented to third parties. Your data will be used for the purpose of this promotion only.

Send completed Voucher form to:
The Francis Frith Collection,
19 Kingsmead Business Park, Gillingham,
Dorset SP8 5FB

Voucher for **FREE** and Reduced Price Frith Prints

Please do not photocopy this voucher. Only the original is valid, so please fill it in, cut it out and return it to us with your order.

Picture ref no	Page no	Qty	Mounted @ £12.00	Framed + £20.00	Total Cost £
		1	Free of charge*	£	£
			£12.00	£	£
			£12.00	£	£
			£12.00	£	£
			£12.00	£	£
			£12.00	£	£

Please allow 28 days for delivery. Offer available to one UK address only

* Post & handling		£3.80
Total Order Cost		£

Title of this book . . . .

I enclose a cheque/postal order for £ . . . .

made payable to 'The Francis Frith Collection'

OR please debit my Mastercard / Visa / Maestro card, details below

Card Number:

Issue No (Maestro only):   Valid from (Maestro):

Card Security Number: Expires:

Signature:

Name Mr/Mrs/Ms . . . .

Address . . . .

. . . .

. . . .

. . . . Postcode . . . .

Daytime Tel No . . . .

Email . . . .

Valid to 31/12/16

Can you help us with information about any of the Frith photographs in this book?

We are gradually compiling an historical record for each of the photographs in the Frith archive. It is always fascinating to find out the names of the people shown in the pictures, as well as insights into the shops, buildings and other features depicted.

If you recognize anyone in the photographs in this book, or if you have information not already included in the author's caption, do let us know. We would love to hear from you, and will try to publish it in future books or articles.

An Invitation from The Francis Frith Collection to Share Your Memories

The 'Share Your Memories' feature of our website allows members of the public to add personal memories relating to the places featured in our photographs, or comment on others already added. Seeing a place from your past can rekindle forgotten or long held memories. Why not visit the website, find photographs of places you know well and add YOUR story for others to read and enjoy? We would love to hear from you!

www.francisfrith.com/memories

Our production team

Frith books are produced by a small dedicated team at offices near Salisbury. Most have worked with the Frith Collection for many years. All have in common one quality: they have a passion for the Frith Collection.

Frith Books and Gifts

We have a wide range of books and gifts available on our website utilising our photographic archive, many of which can be individually personalised.

www.francisfrith.com

Free Print – see overleaf